ECO-DISASTERS

KILLER SMOG

LONDON, ENGLAND

by Joyce Markovics

Consultant: Peter Brimblecombe
Associate Dean and Chair, Professor of Environmental Chemistry
School of Energy and Environment
City University of Hong Kong

BEARPORT
PUBLISHING

New York, New York

Credits

Cover and Title Page, © Trinity Mirror/Mirrorpix/Alamy; 4T, © TopFoto/The Image Works; 5T, © holbox/ Shutterstock; 5B, © Mary Evans Picture Library/Alamy; 6, © TopFoto/The Image Works; 7, © TopFoto/The Image Works; 8T, © Classic Image/Alamy; 8B, © World History Archive/Alamy; 9, © ESB Professional/Shutterstock; 10T, © Sander van der Werf/Shutterstock; 10B, London Smog, 1952 (colour litho), Howat, Andrew (20th Century)/ Private Collection/ © Look and Learn/Bridgeman Images; 11, © The Walters Industrial Archive Heritage Images/ Newscom; 12, © Staff/Mirrorpix/Newscom; 13, Westminster Bridge, London, c.1952 (photo)/ Photo © Brian Seed/ Bridgeman Images; 14T, © TopFoto/The Image Works; 14B, © Keystone Pictures USA/Alamy; 15, © TopFoto/ The Image Works; 16, © PA Images/Alamy; 17, © AP Photo; 18, © John Gay/English Heritage.NMR/Mary Evans; 19T, © Heritage Image Partnership Ltd/Alamy; 19B, © narin phapnam/Shutterstock; 20, © A and N photography/ Shutterstock; 21T, © Arne9001/Dreamstime; 21B, © BSIP/Newscom; 22, © INTERFOTO/Alamy; 23T, © Lebrecht Music and Arts Photo Library/Alamy; 23B, © Iatsenko Olga/Shutterstock; 24, © Trinity Mirror/Mirrorpix/Alamy; 25T, © Pictorial Press Ltd/Alamy; 25B, © ESB Professional/Shutterstock; 26, © melis/Shutterstock; 27L, © Lenscap Photography/Shutterstock; 27R, © Frederic Legrand - COMEO/Shutterstock; 28, © Colin Underhill/Alamy; 29, © rSnapshotPhotos/Shutterstock; 31, © ESB Professional/Shutterstock.

Publisher: Kenn Goin
Senior Editor: Joyce Tavolacci
Creative Director: Spencer Brinker
Photo Researcher: Editorial Directions, Inc.

Library of Congress Cataloging-in-Publication Data

Names: Markovics, Joyce L., author.
Title: Killer smog : London, England / by Joyce Markovics.
Description: New York, New York : Bearport Publishing, [2018] | Series:
    Eco-disasters | Includes bibliographical references
    and index.
Identifiers: LCCN 2017014716 (print) | LCCN 2017022747 (ebook) |
    ISBN 9781684022793 (ebook) | ISBN 9781684022250 (library binding)
Subjects: LCSH: Smog—England—London—Juvenile literature. | Environmental
    disasters—England—London—History—20th century—Juvenile literature. |
    Air—Pollution—Health aspects—Juvenile literature.
Classification: LCC TD883.7.G72 (ebook) | LCC TD883.7.G72 L6644 2018 (print)
    | DDC 363.739/20942109045—dc23
LC record available at https://lccn.loc.gov/2017014716

For more information, write to Bearport Publishing Company, Inc., 45 West 21st Street, Suite 3B, New York, New York 10010. Printed in the United States of America.

10 9 8 7 6 5 4 3 2 1

Contents

The Great Smog

On a chilly, windless day in December 1952, a thick yellowish-black fog settled over London, England. The foul-smelling air was so **dense** people shuffled along sidewalks barely able to see their feet. Rosemary Merritt, a schoolgirl at the time, remembers linking hands with other children to get to and from school. Drivers blinded by the fog inched along the streets, causing huge traffic jams.

The smog was so dense "it's like you were blind," remembers Stan Cribb, a Londoner on his way to work.

Heavy fogs are common in London. However, the yellowish-black cloud that hung over London in December 1952 was different. It was actually a deadly kind of air pollution called **smog**.

To avoid getting stuck in traffic, Rosemary's father walked more than an hour to get home from work that day. When he finally reached the front door, Rosemary remembers, "He was not breathing very well, and coughing quite a lot." That night, when Rosemary was asleep, "I was woken up by my mum banging on doors." Her dad was gasping for air.

A view of the London landmark Big Ben during the 1952 smog

Big Ben on a clear day

A Terrible Loss

In a **panic**, Rosemary's mother called the doctor. However, he couldn't reach their house in the thick smog. With no other options, Rosemary and her mother decided to get the medicine themselves. They walked slowly toward the doctor's office. The **sooty** air made it hard to breathe.

The blanket of smog made the simplest things, such as walking, dangerous.

The Great Smog of 1952 is considered the world's worst air pollution disaster.

Rosemary and her mom finally reached the doctor's office, got the medicine, and made their way home. When they arrived at their house, they were stunned to discover that Rosemary's father had died! Sadly, he was not the only person to lose his life during The Great Smog of 1952. By the time the smog had lifted, thousands of lives were lost.

Looking Back

What had caused The Great Smog of 1952? The story begins in the late 1700s. That's when London became one of the biggest **industrial** centers in the world. Thousands of factories—making everything from glass bottles to fabric—were built throughout the city. In order to power the factories, huge amounts of **coal** were burned. The people of London also used tons of coal to heat their homes and to cook their food.

Coal was inexpensive and readily available throughout England.

Cotton mills and industrial buildings in England in the 1800s.

As London continued to grow over the centuries, more and more coal was used. The burning coal sent giant **plumes** of smoke and tiny particles of soot into the air. It also released dangerous gases. When all of this pollution mixed with fog, it created smog.

London sits in a huge **basin** along the River Thames. It's surrounded by low-lying hills that trap fog in the city.

By 1900, more than four million people were living in London. Many relied on coal for warmth. By 1950, the population had doubled.

Pea Soupers

By the 1900s, more than one million chimneys were pumping coal smoke into London's air. Smog had become a common problem in the city. On some days, it hung in the air like a blanket. Because smog is often very thick and can appear yellowish in color, it can look like pea soup. Londoners would often call a bad day of smog a "pea souper."

Smog can appear yellow, greenish, or very dark in color.

This picture shows a man struggling to breathe during a pea souper.

People with **respiratory** problems were often very uncomfortable during pea soupers. The pollution irritated their lungs, making it hard to breathe. On days when the smog was very bad, the elderly, very young, or sick could become seriously ill when the tiny soot particles in the air **lodged** in their weak lungs. The smog that hit London in 1952 wasn't just any pea souper, though. It was the deadliest smog ever to **shroud** the city.

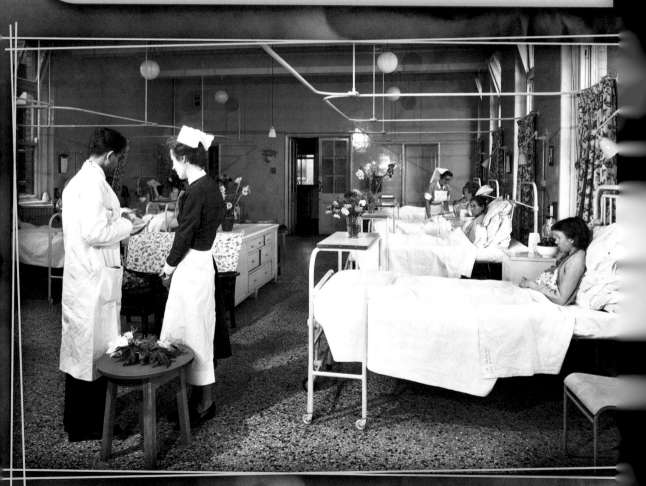

People suffering from breathing problems are treated at a London hospital.

The black soot in the air on a smoggy day caused some people to cough up dark-colored **phlegm**.

December 5, 1952

Friday, December 5, 1952, was a freezing cold day in London. To stay warm, people shoveled extra coal into their fireplaces, creating clouds of thick black smoke. At the same time, coal-burning factories and power plants sent tons of soot-filled smoke into the air. The smoke from the homes and factories contained poisonous chemicals, such as carbon dioxide, sulfur dioxide, and hydrochloric acid. The deadliest chemical—sulfuric acid—formed when sulfur dioxide mixed with the moist London air.

Factory chimneys poke up through the thick smog covering London.

A huge amount of sooty smoke and deadly gases swirled together in the sky. However, instead of rising into the air and spreading out, the cold, windless air trapped the **exhaust** just above the ground. A thick layer of smelly smog formed over the city. By the weekend, Londoners were facing a crisis they never could have imagined.

In some places, the blanket of smog was more than 200 feet (61 m) thick. It was also about 30 miles (48 km) wide!

Blinded!

By Saturday morning, the smog had blocked out the sun's light. Greyhounds running around a racetrack jolted to a stop when they couldn't see the rabbit they were chasing. **Disoriented** birds crashed into buildings. On London's streets, drivers blinded by the smog abandoned their cars and started walking. Double-decker bus drivers pulled over to the side of the road or circled back to the station.

People wait in long lines to climb aboard a double-decker bus.

A goalie strains to see his teammates and the ball in the fog.

As the **visibility** worsened, policemen held flaming torches as a way to guide the vehicles and **pedestrians**. This, however, did little to help. "I had to creep along the walls of the buildings, to the next corner, to read the name of the street," remembers Donald Acheson, a young doctor at the time.

The low visibility caused many accidents. Cars and buses ran off the road. Two trains crashed into each other near London Bridge.

This bus crashed head-on into another bus due to the smog. Eleven people were injured.

Filthy Air

The thick, filthy air also crept into buildings, making it impossible to see. At many of London's theaters, shows were canceled because viewers couldn't see the stage or screen. Nurses at the Royal London Hospital remembered not being able to see from one end of their **ward** to the other.

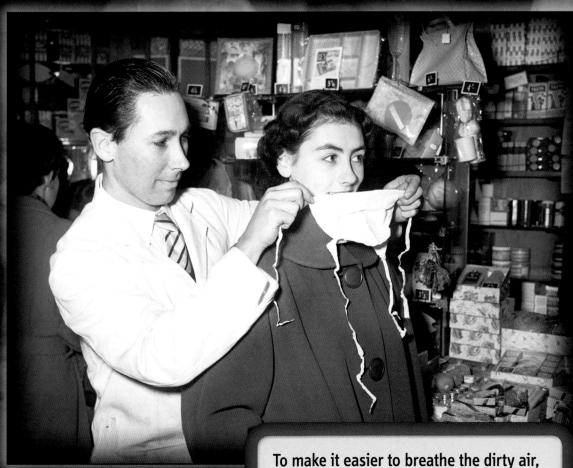

"You blew your nose and black slime came out," remembers a woman who was nine years old at the time of the smog.

To make it easier to breathe the dirty air, some Londoners wore masks. "When my parents went out, they had to cover their nose and mouth with a handkerchief," remembers Londoner Ken Livingstone.

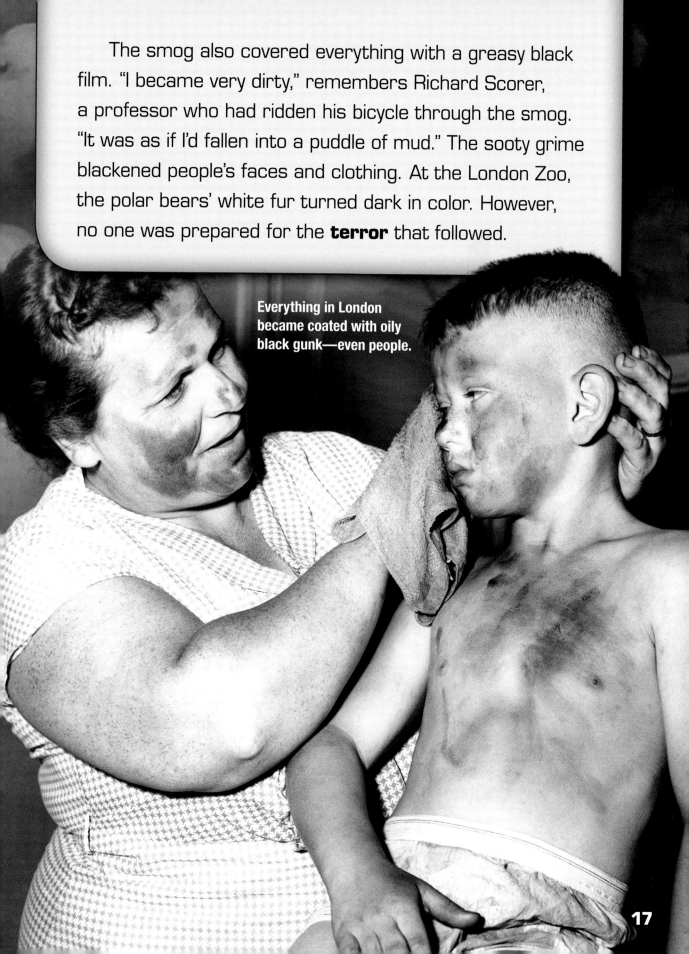

The smog also covered everything with a greasy black film. "I became very dirty," remembers Richard Scorer, a professor who had ridden his bicycle through the smog. "It was as if I'd fallen into a puddle of mud." The sooty grime blackened people's faces and clothing. At the London Zoo, the polar bears' white fur turned dark in color. However, no one was prepared for the **terror** that followed.

Everything in London became coated with oily black gunk—even people.

Sickened by Smog

The smog was more than just a huge inconvenience. At an animal fair, eleven prized cows collapsed after breathing in the **noxious** air. In an attempt to save the animals, the owners tied grain sacks around the cows' noses and mouths. Despite the makeshift masks, the animals still **perished**.

A cow at the Smithfield Club Cattle Show

Around the city, people, too, were dying . . . by the hundreds. Dr. Donald Acheson remembers hospital wards filling with people who couldn't breathe. Without enough clean air and **oxygen**, their lips turned blue. At the hospital, "the supply of oxygen [tanks] was stretched to the limit," remembers Dr. Acheson. By December 6, five hundred people in London had died from the smog.

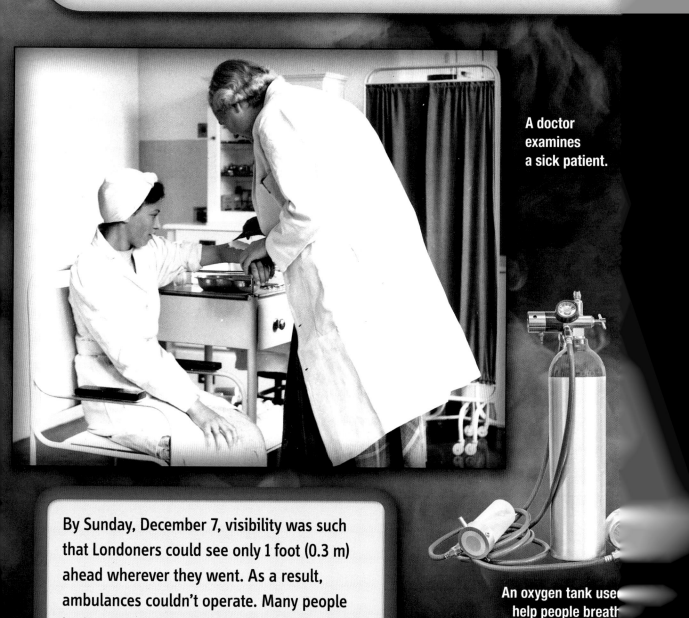

A doctor examines a sick patient.

An oxygen tank use⬤ help people breath⬤

By Sunday, December 7, visibility was such that Londoners could see only 1 foot (0.3 m) ahead wherever they went. As a result, ambulances couldn't operate. Many people had to walk to the hospital through the smog.

Illness and Death

Smokers and people with lung disease were the first to die. They developed serious infections, such as pneumonia. Inside their bodies, pus oozed from their weakened lungs. Over time, as the infections worsened, victims **suffocated**.

The acid in the air burned peoples' throats, causing coughing fits.

It's believed that 100,000 people became ill as a result of the smog.

Then more and more people fell ill. As the days passed, the death rate rose sharply. Soon, **undertakers** began to run out of **coffins** to bury the dead, and florists used up all their flowers. It's thought that as many as 12,000 people died during The Great Smog.

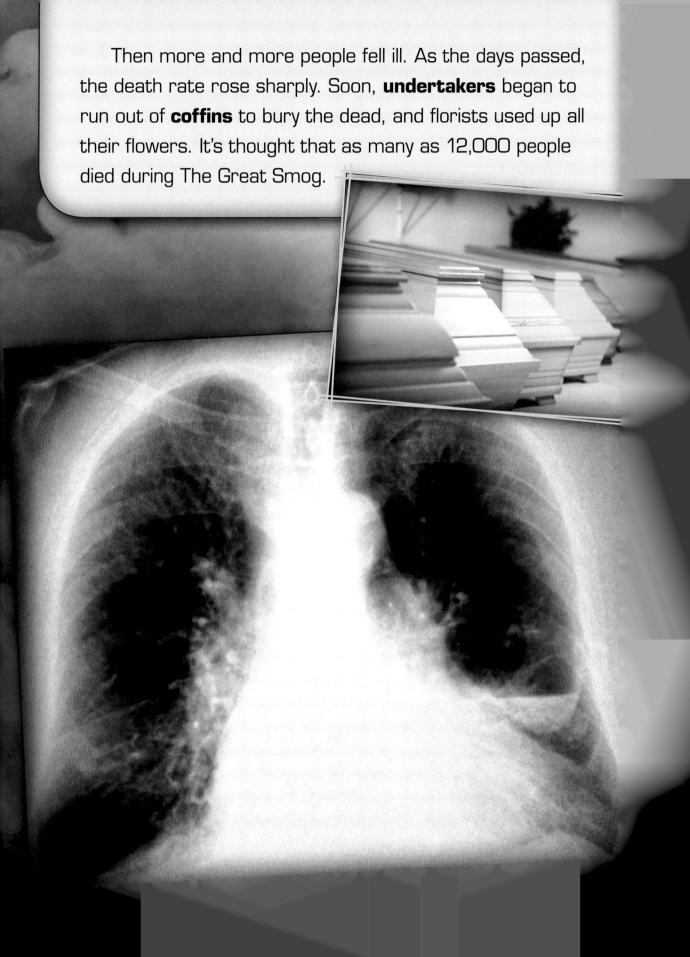

The Great Smog Lifts

Finally, after five long days, a strong wind blew the killer smog out to sea. Then it started to rain. The black sooty grime that was caked on everything was washed away. People could once again see their feet as they walked. Traffic whizzed down the city's streets. Big Ben and other London landmarks shone clearly in the bright sky.

Londoners rejoiced when it rained.

The Great Smog of 1952 lasted from December 5 to December 9.

Things began to return to normal. However, the effects of the terrible air pollution were still being felt throughout the city. People sickened by the smog continued to die. In addition, the smog resulted in thousands of new cases of lung diseases, such as asthma.

People stand among pigeons on a clear day in Trafalgar Square in London.

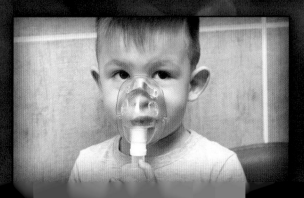

Many people who were children in 1952 went on to develop asthma. This little boy receives treatment for his asthma.

The Clean Air Act

At first, the British government tried to **downplay** the disaster. One government official blamed the weather. He also said that air pollution was a necessary part of life in London. The people of London knew that these claims weren't true. Groups fighting for cleaner air, such as the Coal Smoke **Abatement** Society as well as **politicians**, demanded the government take action.

A woman wears a new anti-smog mask in 1953.

Finally, in response to the disaster, the government passed the Clean Air Act of 1956. New laws encouraged people to burn cleaner fuel that created less pollution. It also set up smoke-free zones in London. Power plants and other polluting factories were required to move farther outside the city, away from people's homes.

A man cooks on an electric stove. Londoners received money from the government to switch to cleaner sources of energy, such as electricity or natural gas.

By decreasing air pollution, the Clean Air Act increased the amount of sunshine in London by 70 percent.

London's Air Today

Despite efforts to reduce air pollution in London, another deadly smog struck in December 1962. However, the number of deaths was a few hundred—much fewer than in 1952. Although there hasn't been another disaster like The Great Smog, air pollution is still a major problem in London.

London continues to have smoggy days.

Experts found that more than 30,000 people are dying **prematurely** from air pollution across the United Kingdom each year. While coal smoke no longer fills the air, much of the air pollution comes from vehicle exhaust. With more than three million cars on London's streets, air pollution continues to put lives at risk.

MAYOR OF LONDON

"Every child deserves the right to breathe clean air," says London's mayor Sadiq Khan.

Air pollution also comes from more than one million wood-burning stoves used throughout London.

Millions of vehicles clog London's streets and pump pollution into the air.

Fixing the Future

Since the 1952 killer smog in London, actions have been taken to prevent air pollution from happening in the future. However, much more can still be done. Here are some examples.

Making the Air Cleaner

- **Diesel** vehicles produce lots of pollution. In 2016, the mayor of London promised new measures to reduce diesel exhaust. He also has plans to put more environmentally friendly buses on London's streets.

- Instead of purchasing diesel cars, people can choose electric cars, which don't release dangerous chemicals into the air.

- Trees and other plants absorb pollutant gases and help filter dangerous particles out of the air. By planting more trees, Londoners can help make the air cleaner.

Standing Up for Clean Air

- An organization called the British Lung Foundation wants the government to ban diesel cars altogether. "Children living and attending school in highly polluted areas are more likely to have damaged lungs when they grow up," said Dr. Penny Woods of the British Lung Foundation. "It's a complete no-brainer: investing in making cycling and walking safer and more accessible in our cities—and moving toward ditching diesel—will not only help clear up our roads, but will clean up the air we're all breathing too."

- Sophie Neuburg of Friends of the Earth is fighting to create no-**idling** zones. "We strongly welcome any action to protect children's growing lungs, and no-idling zones around schools are an important way to reduce children's exposure to pollution."

A sign announces a no-idling zone outside a hospital in London.

Breathing Easier

- Despite the progress being made to make the air cleaner, much more needs to be done. The number of people exposed to dangerous air pollution is growing every year. In addition, the number of early deaths and illnesses from exposure to air pollution is increasing.

- According to one environmental **advocate**, "Sixty years after the killer fog lifted in London, people are dying preventable deaths and suffering life-changing illnesses, simply because they must breathe the air of the cities where they live."

New double-decker London buses emit fewer pollutants into the air than traditional diesel-engine buses.

Glossary

abatement (uh-BEYT-muhnt) the ending or reduction of something

advocate (AD-vuh-kit) a person who supports or speaks in favor of something

basin (BEY-suhn) a low area surrounded by higher land

coal (KOHL) a black rock that can be burned as fuel

coffins (KAWF-inz) long boxes in which dead people are placed for burial

dense (DENSS) very thick

diesel (DEE-zuhl) a kind of fuel

disoriented (dis-AWR-ee-uhnt-uhd) feeling confused

downplay (DOUN-pley) to reduce something's importance

exhaust (eg-ZAWST) smoke and other gases released when fossil fuels are burned

idling (AHYD-ling) operating a vehicle while stopped or waiting, which creates exhaust

industrial (in-DUHSS-tree-uhl) having to do with factories and businesses

lodged (LOJD) stuck

noxious (NOK-shuhs) harmful to one's health

oxygen (OK-suh-juhn) an invisible gas in the air that people and animals need to breathe to stay alive

panic (PAN-ik) a sudden feeling of fright or terror

pedestrians (puh-DESS-tree-uhnz) people who are walking

perished (PER-ishd) dead or destroyed

phlegm (FLEM) a thick substance that can be found in the lungs and is often coughed up when a person is ill

plumes (PLOOMZ) long clouds of smoke

politicians (pol-uh-TISH-uhnz) people who are involved in government

prematurely (PREE-muh-choor-lee) occurring or done too soon

respiratory (RESS-pi-ruh-taw-ree) relating to the group of organs that help a person breathe

shroud (SHROUD) to cover something

smog (SMOG) fog combined with smoke and other polluting chemicals

sooty (SUT-ee) covered with a fine black powder that is made when something is burned

suffocated (SUHF-uh-keyt-uhd) killed from lack of air

terror (TER-ur) something that causes great fear

undertakers (UHN-der-tey-kerz) people whose business it is to prepare and bury dead bodies

visibility (viz-uh-BILL-uh-tee) the distance that an object can be clearly seen

ward (WAHRD) a large room in a hospital used to treat patients

Bibliography

Corton, Christine L. *London Fog: The Biography*. Cambridge, MA: Belknap Press (2015).

Wise, William. *Killer Smog: The World's Worst Air Pollution Disaster*. Lincoln, NE: iUniverse (2001).

Read More

Allaby, Michael. *Fog, Smog & Poisoned Rain (Dangerous Weather)*. New York: Facts On File (2003).

Lawrence, Ellen. *Dirty Air (Green World, Clean World)*. New York: Bearport (2014).

Simons, Rae. *A Kid's Guide to Pollution and How It Can Make You Sick*. Vestal, NY: Village Earth Press (2016).

Learn More Online

To learn more about the 1952 killer smog in London, England, visit
www.bearportpublishing.com/EcoDisasters

Index

About the Author

Joyce Markovics is the author of many
nonfiction children's books. She would like to
dedicate this book to Dr. Sharon Markovics,
who has compassionately committed her life
to helping people breathe a little easier.